Riddles of My Mother

Amos Tabalia

Copyright © **August 2011**

All rights reserved.

This publication may not be reproduced, in whole or in part, by any means including photocopying or any information storage or retrieval system, without the specific and prior written permission of the author and publisher.

This book is sold subject to the condition that it shall not, by way of trade or otherwise, be re-sold, hired out, or otherwise circulated without the author's or publisher's prior consent in any form of binding or cover other than that in which it is published and without a similar condition including this condition being imposed on the subsequent purchaser.

First Edition: August 2011
Published by Nsemia Inc. Publishers (www.nsemia.com)

Edited By: Charles Phebih-Agyekum
Cover Concept Illustration: Abel Murumba
Cover Design: Danielle Pitt
Layout Design: Kemunto Matunda

Note for Librarians:
A cataloguing record for this book is available From Library and Archives Canada.

ISBN: 978-1-926906-09-6

DEDICATION

I dedicate this volume to Maurice and Lynnet Tabalia, the rest of my family and friends. I will on no account overlook what you made me experience. When I thought I was about to go down I kept trying, I had courage when I discovered I need never to fail you, for you gave me the sense of creativity. You would not have stated if I fell apart but you gave me the audacity to hold on. I have for all time heard your voice influence me to do things even beyond my part.

TABLE OF CONTENTS

PART I - AFRICA
1. Motherland --3
2. Prodigal son ---4
3. Africa waiting for the good Samaritan ------------5
4. They caught up with him ---------------------------6
5. Our ways ---7
6. Days of the jungle fire ------------------------------8
7. Immediately after 63 --------------------------------8
8. Africa: I present my case --------------------------9
9. Heroics of our ancestors --------------------------10
10. From the source of wisdom ----------------------12

PART II - POLITICS AND WAR
1. No more gunshots --------------------------------17
2. Another soul dead --------------------------------17
3. Our hero --18
4. I shall not rejoice ---------------------------------19
5. Another lie --20
6. The leaders --21
7. Revolt ---22
8. A living corpse ------------------------------------22
9. War victor or loser -------------------------------23
10. Clouded chambers -----------------------------24
11. Flight to Medina --------------------------------24
12. Clean war ---------------------------------------25
13. Why I fight --------------------------------------26
14. Up the ranks -----------------------------------27

PART III - DEATH AND POVERTY

1. Hunger — 31
2. RIP Great sire — 32
3. Yams everyday — 32
4. Attached to my heart — 33
5. Lost — 34
6. My epitaph — 35

PART IV - RELIGION AND NATURE

1. Above us — 39
2. Before midnight — 39
3. After midnight — 40
4. 2000 anno domino — 41
5. Lucifer — 42
6. The mist — 43
7. Night — 43
8. Sleep — 44
9. Baptism — 45
10. Contract — 45
11. Open gates — 46
12. After Easter — 47
13. Rain — 48
14. A song of praise — 49
15. Twinkling, Dimming — 49

PART V - PHILOSOPHY AND AIDS

1. Another kiss another dead — 53
2. The walking ghost vampire — 53
3. Why the hurry — 54
4. Silence — 55
5. Hope — 55
6. Gone afore — 56
7. Peace — 57

8. Knowledge -- 57
9. AIDS --- 58
10. Binoculars in the heart -------------------------- 59

PART VI - LOVE AND LIFE
1. Still near you ------------------------------------- 63
2. Fading pink --------------------------------------- 63
3. Friendship -- 64
4. Life: from good to bad ------------------------- 65
5. Buried love --------------------------------------- 66
6. Treasured Moments ---------------------------- 67
7. Chronology of life ------------------------------- 68
8. Down the drain ---------------------------------- 71
9. Gateway to my heart --------------------------- 73

PART VII - MISCELLANEOUS
1. Reflections --------------------------------------- 77
2. Like ghouls -------------------------------------- 78
3. This world --------------------------------------- 78
4. I spoke --- 79
5. When Part I ------------------------------------- 80
6. When Part II ------------------------------------ 81
7. Sharia law --------------------------------------- 82
8. US --- 83
9. Soldier cry -------------------------------------- 84
10. Jerusalem -------------------------------------- 84
11. Unfair --- 85
12. Thank you ------------------------------------- 86
13. Little robin hood ----------------------------- 87
14. Baghdad: city of Sinbad -------------------- 87
15. The fall -- 88

ACKNOWLEDGEMENTS

I express my heartfelt appreciation to all who made it possible for me to achieve this fete. To Mrs. Amugune, Ms Ambula and Mr Chetambe, I am indebted to you to a great extent for your support, encouragement and teaching me how to write.

Special acknowledgements to Dr. Tom Odhiambo and the *Amka Forum* for culturing me in this great art, I warmly appreciate you. I have no partiality in expressing my indisputable thanks.

FOREWORD

This anthology of poetry from a young poet that I would like to call a 'poetic toddler' reflects a remarkable re-awakening in Kenyan literature. This collection of poetry comes in the wake of a force fully flowing current of poetic anthologies. Most of these anthologies are by young Kenyan men and women who are not persuaded by the cynicism of many publishers and critics whose refrain is: there is no longer worthy poetry or poets in Kenya. 'No,' this new voices seem to suggest ' We are here and we will sing our songs whether you are ready to listen or not'

Here is an example of this new breed of bold and focused poetic voices. Tabalia's poetry crosses stylistic boundaries, meanders through many themes, and carries the enthusiasm and hope of youth, whilst reflecting the doubt and skepticism of a wide mind. Often his verse reflects anger , anxiety and subtle resignation. But also, as seemingly the young only can be, Tabalia's poetry is about hope, laughter, love, the good in life etc.

Here is a young poet who is aware of what society can and cannot offer him and his generation; a poet sensitive to geopolitics; a voice like many before him and more who will come after him concerned with what means to the human. Can criticism really say anything worthy of art? I doubt. One needs to read these verses and judge for oneself. I can only say that this anthology is a sign of newness in Kenyan literature

Dr Tom Odhiambo
Department of Literature
University of Nairobi

About the Author

Amos Marcel Nyongesa Tabalia was born in Saboti, Trans Nzoia County in 1985 in a family of seven. He was educated in Webuye Town at St Joseph's RC primary School and later joined Friends School Kamusinga where he did his KCSE in 2004. It was while in primary school that he fell in love with literature.

His passion for poetry and other related arts was evident when he joined high school. He started a Readers club that was instrumental in helping other students to grow affection for language and current affairs. He is an avid reader and his mantra, 'To write, read'.

He joined Kenyatta University in 2006 and to the surprise of many, decided to pursue a degree in an engineering course and not in literature as many expected.

Amos is a talented poet who likes to meet new challenges. His works capture themes ranging from the various social, political and economical challenges that a young Kenyan youth experiences. His poetry tries to merge African culture and western influence. His poetry crosses borders and explores the universe. He believes that we are citizens of the universe and we should respect the laws of nature.

His artistic styles are also highly influenced by his childhood experiences, tribal clashes, poverty, wealth, love, education, history, and religion, among others. Tribalism is also one thing that haunted his childhood and corruption are some of the issues that are greatly reflected in his poetry.

He is a founding member of Poetwise Kenya, a group of young Kenyan poets trying to promote the new breed of poets. He is a performer and also a critic at the *Amka - space of women writers*.

His hobbies include interacting and connecting with others over social media, travelling and listening to rock music.

PART I - AFRICA

MOTHERLAND

Where the sun sets
And where it rises
Where I was born
And where I will be buried
When I die away from here
Know that I was on a journey
And was just a visitor
For motherland awaits my body

My grandfather made a journey
To the shores of the great lake
Where animals stay in water
And married a daughter of theirs
For decades long, lived he with them
Until death claimed him back
The heartland called him back
When they buried him
Lightning struck his hut
And carried his skull back

You are lost child of my father
The land of henna calls us back
To till it and make it rich
The illusionary world of the orient
Is not our home child
Blackness is our heritage
Come, build our homeland
Then, they will fear and respect us
If we build the adopted culture
They laugh at us behind our backs.

Our forefathers sung of the motherland
The soil, that holds remains of my ancestors

Calls us back, to live a life
Kiss its earthly wealth
Drink its fresh honey and air
And leave the mechanical life, skyscrapers
Wheels that drive us crazy
Noisy parks that make rest
In the motherland we live a life
And in the city we act a life
The ancestors watch, as motherland waits

THE PRODIGAL SON
Yes
I got my share of you
You moulded me from your flesh
And hardened me from your fire
From you I became a substance

With age and time
I found myself in dilemma
To choose you, my humble background
Or your foes, with flashy life
Needless to say I fell for materialism

Not knowing what lay ahead
I marched with them in their lost ways
As they fed on your toil, your sweat
I ganged with them, hurling insults at you
Not knowing your woe is mine too.
You remained loyal to your cause
And loved me more
When I left you in depression
You waited on me
Knowing well that I will come back.

They drank all that I had in me
And left a skeleton of my old self
 And during distress
Away they ran and left me
As I buckled and sunk on my knees

You took me back with no question
And embraced me with a smile on your face
And cleaned and dressed my wounds
Passionately showing me your love
Like nobody ever showed me before
Ashamed I am a prodigal son

AFRICA WAITING FOR THE GOOD SAMARITAN
Africa
Lying naked on this grass
Your legs sprawled apart
Your open raw wounds filled with stench
Black blood and stench oozes from your bony flesh
And still you await the Good Samaritan

Your own sons
Have run away from you
After letting strangers to suck

Your green fertile fields
And leave a scrape of your old self
But with hope you await the Good Samaritan
Your aim
Reclaim your identity, the brown shiny beauty
The smooth black Valleys
The green plains with the ever flowing river of life
But you hope for this through a Good Samaritan
The same one who reaps your toil
Bringing miseries to you
Africa you are your own rejuvenation

THEY CAUGHT UP WITH HIM

We buried him under the *mugumo* tree
Where his umbilical cord was buried
We buried him facing the mountain
Where our ancestors could talk to him

We wrapped his body in banana leaves
After stripping off the suits and chains
An old man, burnt his fore skin with herbs
And applied charms on his body

The hunters came from the forest
And drums were heard the whole night
As we danced round his grave
Till rain, thunder and lighting colluded

And we knew the ancestors had come
Made him one of them
To haunt and hunt the living
That we can never stop loving them

In the city, civilized and modern
In the village like everybody else
The worshipper of old witches

Who knew not even quarter of his wisdom
To whom he drove every Sunday from church
So when he died the ancestors caught up with him

OUR WAYS
Strange is our land
Where life is misery
For all is bribery
If you want to breathe
And avoid death
Then your pocket matter

The hand that gives
And one that receives
All are cursed with guilt
For darkness they built
A culture of crime

The black of this culture
Eats my race like a vulture
Leading to untold stories
Of murder, theft, rape, sad glories
Locked in files burnt to ashes

If culture is bad
Then this is it
If culture is good
Then this is not
Corruption, the selfish hand

I shan't tolerate
This looming dark shadow
That leads to much injustice
For my hand of righteousness
Will slay this wickedness

DAYS OF THE JUNGLE FIRES

I remember those days
Days of the jungle fires
In the wee hours going to the bush
To chase rabbits and antelopes
As thorns pricked our bare foot soles
And broke from the hardness of the country soil

I remember those days
Running in the forest
Collecting wood for the bonfire
Rubbing the fire sticks together
As we chatted and laughed at silly jokes
Singing as we went dancing round the fire

I remember those times
When we drank directly from the streams
High up in the highlands
From the springs of the purest waters
While collecting honey from the trees
The drums reverberating through the whole land

I long for those days
Walking naked with no fear nor shame
Times when happiness was not bought
And the gods were always happy with us
As we roasted the hares and gazelles
On the bonfire of the jungle people

IMMEDIATELY AFTER 63

I am flattered
In the land of the rising sun
Flows a giant river of life
Going through a green valley

Coming out on a plain of ripe barley
As a waterfall on bulky limestone

Green farms with long stalks of corn
Brown burly healthy bulls with long horns
Uncountable, leaving marks of grass which is torn
Are chased by herdsmen in brown skin coats
And ladies carrying black pots
And together as a nation, they march

Deserts with masses of white sands
Dunes swallowing giant winds
Camels carrying people of all kinds
Settled in the middle of darkness
Shining walls with colours of brightness
Is born, a new black civilization
Black, white, red and green
The flag of independence flies
Amid joyous shouts of triumphs
Praises, promises and prayers made
People happy at a jubilant growth

AFRICA: I PRESENT MY CASE
I am glad
That you passed by my place
Whether you loved it or not
You have seen my case

How was the pothole experience
Did the urchins' hands beg
It's lucky you came back, not mugged
Tell me about the garbage mount that stinks

At the checkpoint, how much was the bribe
Entering the office how much for the doorman

Before helping you, didn't they ask for your tribe
At the end of it all, how much had you parted with

Outside, didn't you meet the jobless
Insecurity, armed rogues protecting citizens
But is it not said, they ain't no jobless
And security is paramount

That is home
Claims of democracy and freedom
Where money has a louder voice than the mouth
And nothing moves unless your pocket is heavy

HEROICS OF OUR ANCESTORS

Legend has it
That my grandma
Was a woman of remarkable beauty
Though beauty didn't matter
But on her list of honours
'Twa's distinct like her hard work

My grandma
Is that woman
That the Arab and Nubian
Told about in their stories
About her heroic deeds
And great fetes

It is said
That she alone
Fought armies with her magic
Sweet deep honey razor voice
That reverberated down valleys and plains
On cold and warm nights

Amos Tabalia

Her voice
Was legend itself
When she sung the warrior enemies
Fell down, one after another
And our hurt and dead fighters
Rose and fought the invaders

Such a woman of great virtue
Was she so blessed
With my wise old granddad
An artistic player of the strings
Also an eloquent speaker
With instincts of a lion

So she sung her poems
As he played his strings
And the field grew green
Peace ruled the lands
Human and beasts
Together survived

They were no ordinary
They had for thousands of years
Lived in peace on our land
Then the white men knocked
And the greed of the people sold them
To their magical toys
So the people forgot the gods
And the Caucasians took the land
My grandpa tried to defend
But his earthly life was lost
From a traitorous priest
Who sold him for an iron horse

FROM THE SOURCE OF WISDOM

The old man lies on his back
His bony hands support his head
As he chews the mumo stick
His snuff box, like his body
Tightly clasped in his right palm

Young man, he says
At least have some taste
Have some taste, and take the best
Choose a wife that will make men
Say you chose with your brains

He coughs, young man
Although beauty lies in your eyes
Choose not one with no manners
That shows steak to your father
And has no shame

He shakes his snuff box
Do not choose a beautiful one
That has porridge for brains
For she will think with her stomach
And you will die with no dime

Neither should you choose
One who is too clever for you
Those other men will eat your yams
Under your own nose without your knowledge
For you will be foolish and weak

Have some taste my grandson
Choose not a boxer, that you be turned to a punch box
Better one that you can sit on

But not too much to hurt
For a little pinching removes childishness

Having said so, do not choose stupid
Do not choose ugly
Do not choose weak
Choose your own taste,
Don't say 'twas grandpa who chose

The old man sighs
And stares at the roof
Suddenly he cracks into laughter
So do I
Add some firewood in the fire
And bring me more brew

PART II - POLITICS & WAR

NO MORE GUNSHOTS
Silence the guns
And let peace prevail
What cannot be attained on the battlefield
Can be found on table
No peace comes from the battlefield
No stable power is borne of war
No to bloodshed
No more butchery
No more cries
 No more fear and tears
No more unmarked cemeteries
Yes for peace
Yes for the new dawn
Let's embrace democracy
Together lets dance
And unite as one
 To celebrate the success of peace
Turn the guns into hoes
Soldiers into farmers
Battlefield to farmlands
And let peace prevail
Never to wither again

ANOTHER SOUL DEAD
Tup! Tup! Tup!
This time we counted seven
Twas in the neighbourhood
Innocent victims
I took my saw to make seven coffins

In the morning
We buried our dead

Police say it was a robbery
Nothing was stolen
All the dead spoke one tongue

Could they have killed for pleasure?
We still can't tell
But surely all from one tribe
The leaders said nothing
But continued to incite the masses

In the middle of the night
Tup! Tup! Tup!
Another soul dead
We protested in the streets
Police shot at us
Another soul dead
And the will for freedom grew strong
To overcome tribal barricades
Hoping for the day
When bullets will protect
And not destroy

OUR HERO
Truly he was great
Even after sleeping on duty
He was great
Even after robbing the widows
He was a hero
After his brutal kills
Still he was our champion

He died and was sainted
Speeches never heard before
Were repeatedly played on radio
His name was on everyone's lips
His enemies and those who never heard of him
Identified with his friendship

The burial was a show
A saint's burial is of less colour and pomp
Even Vatican came by
And people, men and women like sand
Cried and mourned rivers
And say I, were men to go to heaven
By amount of tears shed
Then he occupies his seat next to the creator

A king fell
A prince died, no burial like that
But the man, not known for any good
Was dear to people on his death
His name sung and praised across mountains
And on the third day, the ancestors came
The saint went back to the ancestors
Naked, facing the sun was he buried
And magic all around him

I say praise him not
He who is not to be praised
Say the truth, dead people don't hear
He raped the fertile land of ignorant followers
Say it loud and kill his generation
For truth haunts, and the bad that a man does
Just like the good that he did, lives

I SHALL NOT REJOICE
I shall not rejoice
In the gloom that clouds my village
And the blood that spouts from this spring
That once was live with earthly waters
But now, soiled with the redness of war
The monster that swallows my brothers

The grief that hangs
In the air that surrounds
My bloody scythe and scimitar
That has slain my innocent brother
Who in war turned enemy
Brings no joy to my poor heart

Innocent life lost
Amid joyous shouts of soldiers
Jumping on bodies of fallen hostiles
As they rejoice in their victory
Women, children, hags and dying men
Is what they are proud of killing

We won, we won
Yet I will celebrate not
For my hand spilt the blood of my kinsmen
And innocent brother of mine died
How then will I dine in happiness
My face, should be veiled in woe
And the high God, take me quickly
For I deserve nothing better
Than death

ANOTHER LIE
They drove in sleek sedans
As people on the road cheered
Two onlookers were arguing
Were the limos worth 17 or 18 million shillings?
At the market place a crowd formed
In haste a log formed the platform
Now it was a mammoth crowd
The public addressee system from the nearby church was brought

Uhh uhh we shall build roads
Yeeeeaaaaah! The crowds cheered
We shall bring electricity
We shall fight corruption
We shall.....
The list long I cannot remember the other niceties
Sweet and good usual goodies
People don't like the truth
A few coins were distributed
And the crowd danced composing tunes of praises
As they walked to their cars they smiled
"Stupid idiots five more years of public squandering"
The comforts of parliament awaited them
Same old tricks same old lies

THE LEADERS
Tomorrow, Today and Yesterday
What is the difference?
All exist not
Tomorrow turns to today
Today to yesterday
Yesterday was tomorrow
And all turned to today.

You are the leaders of tomorrow
The old greedy leader never lets go
Promise of nonexistence
That buys time and adds nothing
Why such blatant lie corrupts our minds
I never understand.

Today tomorrow and yesterday are now
A time-line separating the three
Exists not
It's now and now or never

Like soldiers with no armour
We have to fight with our hearts
For we can only change now
And not tomorrow, for tomorrow is not

REVOLT

He came up with a thought
That materialized to a quote
Ears were not pleased with it
As it send shivers down their spine

Another thinker, another thought
That countered the first thought
But his was a law
A selfish law to kill a good thought

The law said "whoever disobeys
This law hangs to death"
And he, that made the quote
Chose freedom in death to prison in life

The body like the heart awakened
And the law was broken
In revolt for their freedom
A kick sending shivers and sense to man

A LIVING CORPSE

A politician in Kenya
A Muslim in the US
A Palestine or Jew in Jerusalem
An Indian or Pakistani in Kashmir
An American marine in Baghdad
A whore in sub-Saharan Africa

A youth in Africa
A woman in Kandahar

And will talk no more
For my pleas fell on dead ears
Tired frustrated and stressed to continue suffering am left

I have seen thieves stealing
But I can say it no more
As I report to the same thieves
In police stations with guns and in uniform

But for how long will this go on
When the time is ripe can't hold this no more
Forth all truths will burst
That will melt this cloud
Freeing me from this chambers

WAR VICTOR OR LOSER
In war, there is no victor
All sides are losers
The death of one man
Is the loss of a whole nation
The winner of a war
Is guiltier than the loser
As he murders more people
One who chooses peace, is wise
While one who goes for war is stupid
Refusing to fight is not to fear
But a humane sign
Aggression is no courage
But a sign of barbarism
And war is only for losers
But war is a necessary devil
That only comes with evil

CLOUDED CHAMBERS

I have laughed
And will laugh no more
For only tears pour from my eyes
As a gloomy past, clouds my eyelids

I have begged
And will beg no more
For my hands are lamed
The kick I received, from the thieving minister hurts

I have talked
And will talk no more
For my pleas fell on dead ears
Tired frustrated and stressed to continue suffering am left

I have seen thieves stealing
But I can say it no more
As I report to the same thieves
In police stations with guns and in uniform

But for how long will this go on
When the time is ripe can't hold this no more
Forth all truths will burst
That will melt this cloud
Freeing me from this chambers

FLIGHT TO MEDINA

Hurriedly he changes his clothes
Shaves his beard
Puts on a priests robe
And the papal cap

Outside, police patrols everywhere
Majestically he marches past them
Visible but invisible. Morons
Their blind sights
Roadblocks all over
Army, police, paratroopers
The omnipresent eye of the dictator
As he enjoys the bumpy ride in the garbage van

Past the checkpoints
As a disguised woman
A black *buibui* covering his face
He boards his flight

I will come back
Like the prophet did
And liberate my homeland
He sighs and relaxes in his seat

CLEAN WAR
Am the soldier
Who refuses to take up the gun
Am the soldier
Who doesn't take arms
But uses my arm to fight

Am the soldier
Condemned for being patriotic
Am the soldier
Who refuses to soil myself with blood
But uses my hand to condemn those who do so

Am the soldier
Fighting the clean war

Am the soldier
Cleaning the dirt from this dirty moron
The injustice that's is their culture

I the soldier
With no mental fear
Fighting with my pen and conscious
Trying to stop this madness
That suppresses the will to live
Creating a fear, of extinction
I sleep with my hand on my heart.
For I don't know when they will strike

WHY I FIGHT

Soldier needs revenge
After they felt glorious
For him nothing is victorious
His heart is still furious
And his mind very curious

Soldier needs revenge
Though they call it loyalty
Him he sees it as cruelty
Why all this brutality

Soldier needs revenge
I know not what I say
But always do I pray
That it shouldn't be play
That turns many into clay

Let me breathe
Let me see reason for my fight
Revenge, is it right
To fight other peoples war
Revenge that I know not about
While my little wars go unfought

UP THE RANKS
On the head of the ladder
I stare down at its feet
I plan not to go down
For am at my destiny

We rose through the ranks
We stooped low before
Won favours and hearts
Of masters with dirty baggage

We rose through the ranks
Through good and bad means
The way was painful
Rougher and rougher steeper and steeper

We rose up the ranks
As we watched friends and foes fall
But we never looked back
We kept our heads high towards the sky

We rose up the ranks
Through short and long ways
On the back of gullible admirers
Whom we fooled with our grandiloquent speeches

Same voices that sang our praises
Cry for our heads, but we will not concede
If it takes lives
We have to stay up
Because we can't fall back
To the dirty murk of the ground
Because we rose through the ranks

PART III - DEATH & POVERTY

HUNGER

With pity I look at them
Kids with hungry eyes
Mothers with no shelter
Granny's with no teeth

The children cry
Dry tears
Bodies with no water in them
Like the dried earth under their feet

A woman carrying mangoes
A delicacy that only exists
In these wilderness of nothingness
Water to boil also lacks

My son
The old woman shrills
Stretching her hands at me
I look into her hollow eyes
And anger grips me

Am torn apart
As she falls down on my knees
The wind stops blowing
Everything comes to a standstill
It's quite
No one cries
Energy too, lacks
The strike of hunger
Brutally claims her

R.I.P GREAT SIRE

My life without you
Is a wall with a big hole
A void that will never be filled
Such a humble and humane being
I live to remember you
And your kingly mind

You led me out of darkness
And gave me food and clothing
For you found me in poor state
Fighting with dogs for crumbs of grain
Stranger as I was
You threw a feast for me, like a lost son
You're household, poor in material
But rich in life
A blessing to me it was
With no remorse in your heart
You dressed my wounds and washed my body
Hospitalized me back to form
Sire without you, I am incomplete
Rest in Peace Great Sire

YAMS EVERYDAY

Mummy, yams yams everyday
Roasted yams, one among seven
Yams, dry yams, once in a day
But everyday, yams, yams, yams oh heavens

We live in a trash pit
Outside a ministers mansion
Which is brightly lit
With dogs for protection

Amos Tabalia

The dog, a big animal calf
That feed on special diet
Their cost only half
Can keep for a month, my stomach quiet
My son, we eat a yam
Yams everyday and not ham
For ham is for rich man
And yam is for poor man

Let the dogs be treated like humans
And the poor men live like beasts
Let them clean their dogs with water
While we pick our jiggers with thirst

But one day, our throats will be quenched
As our stomachs will surrender the grumbles
And it will be no yams everyday
But its you son who holds the key

ATTACHED TO MY HEART
Attached to my heart
Is a picture of you
With your radiant face
Smiling at the world

Attached to my heart
Is the memory of that day
That dreadful day
That I learnt what death is

When I found you
Lying prostate in the living room
I thought you were sleeping
Only to be told you were gone

I was so small
And never understood
 Why people were crying
When you were sleeping, resting

They put you in the grave
Then father told me you were gone
Not to wake up again
That's when I cried, cried hard

Death, selfish, unkind robber
So brutal, so merciless
To take away, my only love
My sweet old grandma

Attached to my heart
Are those lovely memories
Which like the sun, shine in me
But soon very soon, I will come

LOST

He died too young
Before the world could tap
His rich brains
We read it in papers
And we couldn't believe it
Two doors from his cottage
Was a man who had seen
The best of the days on earth
And suffered the long wait
Of eternal rest, that never come
But it skipped him
And knocked on this boys door
No sooner had he opened
Than a bullet knocked him down

"He died too soon"
The epitaph on his grave reads

MY EPITAPH
When the lord asks for me
Forget this not
That I tell you
For it has to be done

Plant a mango tree
On my grave, as my epitaph
Plant not a birch tree
As it's only beauty but no fruit

Let it not in words
Or letters say
But its physical stillness
Proclaim my goodwill

Make it grow big
For women with pots, children from play
The tired traveller on his pilgrimage
Provide shade from the heat above

Let this tree be fertile
And its fruit ripe to yellow
That all can enjoy last
From my jigger infested rotting body
And my soul watches in satisfaction

PART IV - RELIGION & NATURE

Amos Tabalia

ABOVE US
There is someone for you and me
All the times he looks at you and me
He can neither be seen nor be heard
But needs respect and not to be feared

His feelings are stronger than love
He is great, but humble like a dove
Always puts trouble to flight
Mine and your enemies He fights

He is great and good
Indeed, he is better than food
His water sweeter than honey
Casts all problems with no money

Someone that   wipes away dark stains
And always paints your heart with joy
Brings happiness even in troy

If you want to win
Pray and commit not sin
So that Satan can recoil
As success comes to you with no toil

BEFORE MIDNIGHT
Clouds gather
As heaven darkens and blackens
Darkness sets in
The road is unseen
No end to the dark tunnel

The countryside is quiet
No crickets and birds to chirp

Lighting a fire proves futile
And evil smells in air
A time of darkness
Towards midnight
Swindles planned and executed
Knives slash living flesh
Houses broken and torched
Witches rule the night

Before midnight
This nation withers
Only dead lame dead projects move
Black businesses make millions
And poor hungry people struggle to choose the best death

AFTER MIDNIGHT

Clouds move away
The moon is high
Stars sparkle the night sky
The early birds chirp
A torch of life from far

Amos Tabalia

The clock ticks its journey
And the cock crows
From far the horizon wakes up
Dawn approaches fast
As souls awaken to another day

Darkness gives way to the sun
Hope amongst the people
And the path is clear
The star of success
Shines on a people hardworking

After midnight
Light illuminates our hearts
Hope guides our efforts
Our nation, at last, reborn
Take the hoes and till the earth

2000 ANNO DOMINO
During darkness
There are those
Who stayed by riverbanks worshipping waters
Others bowing to the sun, moon and the stars
Those who moulded clay and carved stone and wood
Praying to bronze and sculptures
The condemned who believed in mortal things.
When light came
Still, there are those in ignorance
Who stayed on and asked guidance from dead men
Living in memory of myths and legends
And still kept their mountain temples
Sacrificing animals and human beings
The learned who cheered old unwise men

And then the son came
The sun shone brighter
As they listened to the voice from him
And the words came from above
Whose words are everlasting peace
The immortal one with love
Came to save us all

Still there are those
Who turn Christianity to business
And from it try robbing God
Others think it's a way of life
More take it like a comedy act
Those who have a ticket to the bowls of hell
And I say its faith a strong believe

LUCIFER
He is free
Roams the plains and valleys of earth
Moves about oceans and seas
Can't be tamed by mortal laws
 Reaps open flowers undeflowered
Merciless to all with weakened hearts
Forces open closed doors
Steals happiness from others
Sends shivers of terror to all
Takes form in men with no faith
In the most high
Feels an innocent woman
Child or hag can't differentiate
He, the one cast away
From heavens where he was rebellious
And fallen he from sky
To the depths below sky and earth

Because He that liveth was angered
And he is now doomed
To the boughs of hell

THE MIST
Days of dryness are past
And the chilly morn is cast
The dew that kills is born
As farmers prepare their corn
For those who are keen
The coastline is not seen
The mist covers the land
But rain is at hand
The land is calm
As the farmer waves his palm
 Rain has not yet come
Lets go back home
The mist is no rain
But a curtain that kills the grain
The mist is a blindfold
That brings down the bold
As they try to farm
And to their crop does harm

NIGHT
Noble night
Make me sleep
And get not nightmares
For mine skin tickles
Whenever thy ghouls face
Show in mine dreams

The good old devil
From Babylon land

With barbaric blood of Jezebel
Give me peace
And minds rest
So that Satan dies

Mine honour lies on mine sword
I'll slew your throat
And let evil blood pour
To appease mine hurt heart so that rest my kindle
My heart to live long

Night
That makes men evil
Thieves and thugs alike
Rapists that raid
And those that die hard
From drink and darkness sins
Relieve me

SLEEP
Sleep like cops
Makes arrest of this corpse
Stars engulf his core
As his head weighs more
His beauty leaves our empire
As his body changes to a vampire
Eyes close, mouth shut
Face wrinkles ears collapse like a falling hut
And the yawn of a hog
Exposes the tired grin, of a hungry dog
The hands come up
And the head goes for a slap
And the weight is for clown
As the head slumps, crashing down
Shock disbelief confusion charms

Engulf him as he tries to come to terms
Then the yawn is broken
And the hand stretches to awaken
And the arisen master
Is alive after a brief interlude with monster

BAPTISM
Born and named
To live in this world
But still with traces of Adam's sins
And in addition worldly sins
That loses all purity
A cleansing, a rite is eminent
To wash away sins
Reborn, renamed
Anew liberated, rejuvenated
That's what it does
But still no glimmer of hope, change
Like a wind that wipes and promises
Baptism isn't making it new
But remember the world watches

CONTRACT
A contract, agreement between master and servant
And only holds for the stated period
Many breech this contract of life
And it expires before maturity

So is life
A contract between God and man
That finds man breaking the laws in sin
But God doesn't terminate it
Gives man more chance to live

Death is a marker
To the end of this contract signed at birth
In death, more space is created for others to live
So man has to rejoice and celebrate death
And not to mourn others

God will call us
To say our deeds on the last day
So that he can see if we honoured
The contract of life on earth

OPEN GATES
Knock, knock, and knock
Who are you
I am lost with no where to sleep
Come in

Knock knock knock
What can I do for you
I have hungered for three days
Come in

Knock knock knock
Who are you
A runaway wife with an infant
Come in

The church
Opens its gate at all times
To Christians and Muslims
Indians and pagans
Blacks and whites
All alike are welcomed

Amos Tabalia

During the Rwandan genocide
The Vietnamese war
The apartheid struggle
The tsunami rash
Terror attacks, floods and hurricanes
The gates remained open

But they only go there
In times of hardness
Disaster and distress
When problems force them
Still God does not complain
The gates are open to all

Hail Him who is high
He remembers his children
During times of distress
Offering them shelter
Food and clothing
And peace

AFTER EASTER
After Easter, and its partying
The poor went back to their hunger
The rich suffered its hangovers
As those who had fasted, grew fat

Nine months later
The bellies of the young girls
Who offered cheap enjoyment
Bust forth with new life

After sometime
People grew thin and thinner
And we buried some more
The unlucky hosts of the virus

After Easter
Others waited for Christmas
For another chance to church
Or the perennial visit to their homes

After Easter
There are those, who, like before
Saw nothing of importance in it
To them, just another social date
As they continued tending their fields
Preparing for the next harvest

RAIN
When will the scorching sun
Stop burning our fields and forests
When will this sun, stop killing
Our animals and children from hunger

When will dark clouds cover
The blue sky with their shadows
When will the small torrents
Fall down, bringing down streams of hope

When will the rumbles and flashes
Of thunder and lightning come
When will the bare ground
Be green with lilies and blooming roses

We ask for rain to fall
So that we can live and see another season
We ask for rain, but not too much of it
To wipe us out of this world with floods

We ask for rain
Enough to let us go to our fields

And till the land, so that we can sow
And harvest, as we feed nations

We ask not for Noah's catastrophe
Let not the seas open their banks
Or the heavens lift their curtains
And swallow us alive for our sins

A SONG OF PRAISE

Oh precious is the day
Oh precious is the way
So early will I say
For the sun and its ray
To turn grass to hay

Oh let us be the pride
That will heaven ride
For Christ will be our guide
That sends Satan to hide
For us with Christ to abide

Join me by this side
If you don't want to slide
From this carriage and glide
To fall in fires wide
And suffer in red hot hell

TWINKLING, DIMMING

It's early in the evening
The clouds gather
My steps move faster
A pauper like me, where to

Suddenly, large torrents fall
Icy hailstones from nowhere
My tattered clothes can't hold
So I wrap my hands round my chest

I can't run for I have no strength
Four days without a bite
My bare feet tickle painfully with jiggers
Be a pauper then you discover water is expensive

I head towards the verandah
But the women and children make fun of me
Go away you stinking madman
Slowly I crawl back to my stoning bath

I walk in circles in the rain
Not thinking for no strength have I left
I look up and smile at the downpour
As the lightning strikes its sword blow

I fall on my knees, closing my eyes
As the small rivers carry me
And darkness engulfs me
Then from far I see a bright shining light.
This must be purgatory, I sigh in relief.

PART V - PHILOSOPHY & AIDS

ANOTHER KISS ANOTHER DEAD

Girls in pink and red skirts
Others in white and blue trousers
Boys in yellow and green jeans
Others in sagging shorts
Kinky clothes from backstreet designers

Smoke and smell of alcohol
Litter the air with used up condoms
The music loud destroying ears
As they seriously jerk their bodies
In funny movements of their confused music

In corners, in pairs
A boy and a girl not more than 16
A kiss on the mouth then everywhere
I close and open my eyes
Another kiss, another death
A statistic entry to the HIV records

THE WALKING GHOST VAMPIRE

She hailed from the south
Some say she came from the north
But still she was in our midst
Beautiful and young, skilfully moulded

Man she was there
A piece of natural beauty
A girl of high esteem
Leaving us with no otherwise but to fall for her

Was it her long slim legs
Or her big green eyes

With her tan brown skin
That made as fall for her

Yet she was the devil
Such perfect model a murderess
She strangled, not once, and wondered off
From East to West to fulfil her appetite

WHY THE HURRY
Great haste makes great waste
The habits of youth brings no rest
To the nature of our future
For habit is second to nature

Our ways are no longer safe
As the world is not kind
But brings us this fear
That makes our future shear

Is it the anger of the gods Or not?
Or the inversion of the lords
That stakes our youthful days
For those who love pleasurable plays

I console the grief stricken
But amid sobs I see the provocative
Whose looks wipe away the innocent
Who will do anything for little cents

A sure way of suicide
That your skeletons lie by your bedside
So he signed his death
And others blame the gods' wrath

Why, why the hurry
Why hurry and then worry

Don't try it, go slow
And you will have it all

SILENCE
Silence the king is about to enter
Silence is power
With it order is brought
Its mentions and everyone to a standstill
So is concentration born

Silently I write this loud poem
Like a Buddhists monk on his mantra
I silently watch the ocean and think
'Silence is essence'
Moments pass as time ticks by silently

Before the casket is lowered
Silence with the deacons blessing
The judge enters the courtroom
And silence prevails
Silence walks with power

Silence is wisdom
Courageous men, remain silent
Hot iron brands their patriotism
Silent vessels carry treasured cargoes
And the dead are feared for their silence
Silence is fear, silence is courage

HOPE
Behold life paradoxes
While they laugh and make merry
I am sulking, crying and feeling sorry
While they feast on sweetness of honey

Riddles of my Mother

I enjoy the bitter brew that is my brandy
As I strive to get a crumb of bread
Comfortably they feed on chunks of cows dead
As I walk naked in the outside cold
They walk in warm clothes covered in gold
And say they, all humans are equal
And say I, that am not factual
For I know that if on earth there is no paradise
Then in heaven it's not when one dies
But still, the sun never closes it eye
And human being, truth, never hides
For time is coming, when their reign will be over
Today I am the one and tomorrow, them to hover

GONE AFORE

In memory of William Wordsworth
And the likes of Alfred lord Tennyson
Not forgetting Ralf Waldo Emerson
This power of the hand
From Edgar Allan Poe to Emily Dickinson
From Elizabeth Barret Browning
To Christina Georgina Rossetti

From Edna St Vincent Millay
To Henry Reed
I salute you with this pen of mine
And ask for your blessings on my works
So that my limbs may grow stronger
To condemn the bad to the noose
And liberate, the innocent bound by society

PEACE
The original quality of the self
In its purest form, it is the inner silence
That consists of positive thoughts and pure feelings
Good wishes that promote happiness
To have peace you need patience
Creating an atmosphere of peace is peaceful
Peace in the world can only be realized
When there is peace in the minds of men

KNOWLEDGE
As you grow, so you become
What you are meant to be
From the little angel that you were
To the fiend that turns out to be

I was a kid and wiser
Times when life's complications
Hadn't clouded my youthful brain
And I knew not yonder the borders of home

Grandfather used to come
And I tickled his whiskers
My cousins used to visit
And we play with no discrimination

Now am grown
And laughs no more with little ones
I am no longer fond of my grandpa
But instead, resent my village folks
Is it because of this knowledge
In books beyond our black borders
That make me think am learned
That I deserve the respect of the elders
That I am of better class and caste
That I am well bred and nurtured
For the village to say I am great
When they are the better ones
For this knowledge is a confusion of mind

AIDS

A blessing to mankind
Buries men quicker than swords
The wrath of gods on man
To rid the world of sinners
Keeps population from ballooning
Creating more job opportunities
Pretending fraudsters turned saviours to swindle
Keep doctors busy in labs trying to strike gold

Opportunity for the west to trample Africa
Offers poor relatives to grab dying widows
A sweet topic for politicians looking for votes
Medicine men with their concoctions are back in market
And the church to make more money
AIDS what have you done to us?

BINOCULARS IN THE HEART
Societal life is a humongous ball
There are so many whys, queries
And equally many because excuses
Answers that leave me ignoramus

Why is it that beautiful girls
Are always very foolish
Because women worship beauty
And not brains

Why is it that ladies prefer beauty
Not brains
Because men prefer seeing
And not thinking

In their hedonistic beliefs
Why is it that bright girls
Marry lurid and stupid men
Because nature has to balance
Why is nature so selfish
Because it is incessant and purview
And loves to live man in quandary
When itself is a semblance

VI - LOVE & LIFE

STILL NEAR YOU
Perhaps the stars, perhaps the moon
Can tell this story
Nothing ever goes from my memory
Still I think of that glory
We shared when it was a happy story

The lonely days after you were gone
The sleepless nights when I was alone
Weeks and months so cold to the bone
Your ghost still lingered like a clone
Nothing moved me away as we were one

I still feel your gentle arm
Wrapped around my body to make me firm
How will I forget those moments so warm
Still I feel the emptiness and harm
Of staying alone on this big farm

Why did you go alone to clove?
You could have told me my little dove
So that we can go together above
And be bound in eternal love

FADING PINK
A gun in one hand, a rose in another
She, my worst nightmare stood
I've done so much wrong and right
How will I flip the two faced coin
Throw the rose and make me lame
Give the rose and you will have done the same
Don't make me cry o lady
And kneel down on the dust my body
Throw the gun and give me the rose

Throw the rose and shoot me
I will not lose
Life has never been cruel like this

Black rose, black rose, black rose
Darkest night never changed a bit
Never learnt how to love
Never got to feel the warmth
Never got a shoulder to lean on
How come, I never seem to understand?
Never let me touch you
What's so hard, to love or to be loved
That you carry these two to me, when I try
And which is for me, the gun or the rose

My heartaches are growing stronger
My fear raises blood rushing to my head
My hands tremble with fever
Why this day of all days
When I try my charms on you
You raise a gun and a rose
The rose or the gun, which is for me
Throw the gun and give me the rose
So that ours can be another love story
Not gone sour

FRIENDSHIP

Our amity is not spurious
But it is so much veritable
 A condign of no aspersion
But willingness of love to show

What passes through you
Is what will pass in me
When you sulk and life is bad
Then I also feel sad

I say you are so good
Even when not in mood
At times we crisscrossed
But along the bridge we crossed

Friend you're great to me
You and me are there for each other
Our losses to share
And victories to enjoy

LIFE: FROM GOOD TO BAD
Walking down the street
After a heavy day
You need a treat
An evening so gay
Something good after working all day
Marching home, your head held high

Walking with compassion
Home waits with passion
And with a little fashion
To the winds you throw caution
Find yourself in a cafe
Bottle after bottle money from the safe

There is no need for booze
Try and you will see everything ooze
Your wife doesn't like a drunk
Son and daughter their hate frank
When it dawns,
Still you aren't sober
At noon, your boss comes, you have no cover

Your company will have you fired
Nobody will have you hired
That's when trouble will come
Money is not at home
Saying you is no freak
You try other houses to break

Back you hit the streets
Yours becomes crime and trick
But cops with their guns and bullets
Will bring you down
And have you in jail
That's when I say
Life moves from good to bad

BURIED LOVE
Broken smiles, have never been a beauty
Your tears, makes my life so dry
And my heart swells with gloom
Sadness like a dumped up groom

I had a wish to make you mine
But everything never went fine
I had a chance to give you love
But never did I have the courage from above

I hope that you will know
Your going was a big blow
For you was always the red of my soul
Since then my love has never been whole

Once I dreamt of nights with you
Cuddling and fondling you
Now nothing remains of that dream
To have you with me in my rim

Now it's too late
For me and you ours is a sealed fate
Coming back when there is someone bright
Who makes my life come to light

Remember all that hurry
You couldn't wait to listen to my sorry
When I cried for your passion
But out you went for fashion
It's too late, ours is sealed fate

TREASURED MOMENTS
Slowly she reached for me
With a strange movement bringing agony
And a slow insinuation of a kiss
That touched the core of my heart

I had her in my arms, obliterated kissing her
And 'twas sheer, blenched agony in me
She was there, small and light accepting
Like a child with such an insinuation of embrace
Infinite embrace that I could not bear to stand

Then I slept, sealed in the darkest utter sleep
Extreme oblivion, for a few seconds
From which I gradually came
Holding her warm and close to me
Silent in the same oblivion
The fecund darkness was she

Gradually I returned, newly created
A new birth, in the womb of darkness
Aerial and light everything was
New as a morning, fresh and newly begun
And like dawn, the newness and the bliss came in
As I took back control of the game

She bent down, kissed my lips
And dawn blazed on me our new life had come
Beyond all conceiving, it was all good
Almost like passing away, trespass
That leads to a garden of roses
So delicate, but so sweet
That I had to pluck one for myself
That our union

CHRONOLOGY OF LIFE

The undying man is dying
The immortal one is no more
Oh sorrow, all is sorrowful
As the body is about to die
But the soul, lives on
The immortal part that lives
To tell this thorny tough tale

Need I expose to vulgar sight
Raptures of the night conceived
Need I intrude on mine conception

Or draw curtains closed around
But let it suffice that the immortal one
Was born from mortal flesh of man and woman

Listen to me, houseless child of want
That black morn I dropped on this earth
Dark black world I saw and cried
For prophesies I made still young
Of life's great miseries and sorrows ahead
And nigh on this blessed night I'll go back high

Mine childhood was all cheers and venial
With plays gamed till dusk from dawn
O memory thou fond deceiver
To form joys recurring ever
And turning all past pleasure to pain
In mine last hour of tales from brain

Beautiful, beautiful this place earth is
Youth is such a time for pleasure
Alcohol that grime painful experience of leisure
Laughter, merrymaking and fun is what life is
But it's too early for you or you will be knifed
And stumble, fall or drawn lest you are careful

Education for a life full of deluge
Scholars said about the garish hogwash joke
For its few esoteric men gone afore
That know it is sad and puts you to yore
When they learn about the coon
Who is not as the orient think a loon

And life compelled I, to be political
Contenting a depredative regime
In secretion I was branded dissident
With minacious influence on the public

With no trial and fairness, I was detained
And spurious charges of murder brought on me

At the end of this dark tunnel
A room not more than two metres square
With precious darkness, so I do share
Light I saw ten years gone
And night or day I can't tell
But for the three cm hole 120 metres above

Excrement, urine, sweat blood and tears
Flavour my quarter cup ration
And for ten years mine eyes have wandered
In darkness like a cat, to get a glimpse of light
As three drops quench my flaming throat
In my last hours on this earth

They say I killed
And so I face death by the noose
But dying isn't punishment, it's what I long for
For hell torture not more than this world
Why beings pain their fellows so much
That trying to do right sends you to death

In the morrow, they will come for my marrow
And cuff my hands with heavy gongs
My heart will be at peace
And the priest will step forward
As they strap me on the chair
Ready for my salvation to the heavens
And my heart will join angels and legions
At last, my freedom, through death will be nigh
But my spirits, even in death, will smile, alive, to fight
For justice

DOWN THE DRAIN

Can the smooth silvery sky
Or the beautiful blue sea
Echo red romantic lines
Sweet sentiments of my love
Better than my heart

My dearest sweetheart
Do I look like a bastard
Who hears and pretends not
To the princely declarations
Of your love to me

My fairy queen
Why do you look sad
Has it occurred to you how mad
On seeing the calm crystalline eyes
With so much pain,I feel

Its pity that I harbour for you
You and your kind
Whose love lies in their eyes
From what they see
And not what lies yonder

Do I not carry enough riches
To make you a better life
The gifts that I give
Do they not show enough
Of what I harbour for you

Presents keep friendship warm
But they can't buy love
For it can't be measured
In limos,nor gold rings
Unless its lust not love

Call me lusty
Or a hungry sex dog
But my precious dear
There is nothing to fear
Even when you lash at me

Your love I doubt not
But please understand
Prevention is better than cure
Why dig your own grave when you are so young

Why why honey
True love never grows old
I can't abandon you
Even when threatened with death
For beyond this life, my love stretches

If you insist, I will not resist
If you persist, I can't desist
But remember fortune favours fools
Who close their ears, to death calls
I yield, and wield to you this bitter fruit

Calling me names, won't help
For now, rests my souls with pleasure
This gift that you've given me
So sweet with leisure
Confirms our blossoming love to all

You don't know what you're in
You begged for the wrong love
And I donated not love but death
A rose between two thorns
A withering tulip, to fall of the tree

My choice of love I regret
The forbidden act consummates me
I insisted and persisted, when I was warned
And now staggeringly I carry my own cross
Across a sinking bridge in the ocean

Red is the colour of romance
So is also a symbol of danger
Love or lust, serves me to the grave
An honourable life, a cheap death
And outside AIDs continues to stalk
Mankind down the drain

GATEWAY TO MY HEART
You, the mauve and red flower
You the smoked salmon deeply marinated in lemon
You the pink rose popping up in spring
You like a mutton sandwich wrapped in cheese
You the most beautiful red sunset sinking into the sea
You the moonlight sonata quietly seeping out of a piano
You the wild music of the marshy rushes
You the peach juice stained around my mouth
You're the gentle breeze ruffling my scruffy hair
You're the sunlit diamond that abhors above
You're the sweet smell of burning myrrh
You're the emerald city that twinkles in my eye
You, with the soft smooth flowing silvery silk hair
Is the uncopied key to the gateway of my heart

PART VII - MISCELLANEOUS

REFLECTIONS
Listen to the sweet sibilance of my sentences
Listen to the soft soothing tone of my tongue
The sweetness to the dainty dirge of life
That is mirrored in my malachite mind
And carefully carried by mortal hand
To be sketchily scribbled by my precious pen
On a patchy piece of platinum paper

Reflections of life paradoxes
Easy unwieldy hard life
That cajoles and leads man

Reflection of good
And evil found on one earth
That tarnishes mankind's freedom

Reflections of victories
And failures won in the world
That everybody has to pass through

Reflections of great works
That mock bad life
Leaving many lacking happiness

Of the devil and his evil
Sneaking on man in darkness
To cause havoc and haunt

Of sins and dreams
Brutal and grander to many
That some die, so that others can live

These are the reflections
Of poor and rich
Men and women
Wise and foolish
Evil and good
Dead and alive
All in one package
The earth of black and white
King and subject, the two castes

LIKE GHOULS
Black sardonic smiles
Sagging faces with flies
Standing in straight piles
Carrying heavy tiles
Kamiti prison ghouls

All times I ask why
Courts make people fry
And they tell me to try
Say the truth and I will cry
As judges never been just

Like Bakersvile prison look
Cares not between thugs and man of book
As long as you are on the hook
You'll join the living ghouls and brook
In jail where men rote to ghouls

THIS WORLD
Once I was a king
Now am nothing
Once I was a prince
Now I live on chance

Once she was a slut
Now a nun she is but
Born she a virgin
Died a prostitute of sin

The world
Like clay into pots
Once had green plants
But now its fine sands

Now day now light
Nothing is yours on earth
Today you have tomorrow you don't
For fate's best formulae
Is that it has no formulae

I SPOKE

Atomic bombs
Mass murderers
Aided by human speakers
Freezing, turning
Heading back
Lives saved as I spoke

Messages in tinted glass
Lighting up the dark coastline
Its beauty marvelled at
Packages of messages passed
From mouth to mouth
In successive generations
Beautiful beautified words
From past to present

A clean cut prophecy
A dry sullen dirge
Telling of a love story
Or another hero
A buzz on the ear
A sting on the nostril
Jolts of lighting of a scream
And the source in speech

A bejeweled gift
Granting the rich masters desire
A woman-most easily acquired
Freedom-on the table facing each other
Luxury- the gullible spoke with the right people
Power-audience applauded his addressee
White lies clothed in dark truths of sweet words

Give a poor man
And his treatment
Paralysis
Hunger grief
Lost love
On air
Speech. Jewelled gift

WHEN PART I
I am looking forward
To the day when the white
The day when the black
The day when the red
And all the yellows
Will come as one
Put their hands together
And shout out aloud
"United we stand"
We shall move the mountains

We shall move the seas
And make our world
A better place to stay
A world with no fascism
A world with no tribalism
A world with no war
A world with no disease
A world that is free
A world that is alive
To conquer all the space

But when?
When will we see
When will we make
When will we free
Our world from these chains
And attain full freedom

WHEN PART II
When will she wash the dishes
When will she wash the clothes
When will she clean the house
When will she cook the food

When will she collect the firewood
When will she give birth
All the time she cries
Weeping for her freedom
Freedom to roam with men folk
Freedom for indecent clothing
Freedom to contradict her husband
Freedom, freedom from what

Should I sit and look at her
Watch her sell her body
Watch as she grows stronger than me
Watch her patronize my duty
And embarrass me in public

What will make me stop her
Should I punch her
Or place her in her traditional niche
Or just give her the freedom
That she so much yearns for
So that I can now be caged

SHARIA LAW
Man's weakness is staying alive
An adulterers Achilles heel is his eyes
For a thief, it is his hand
A spy's problem is his ears
A rapist, his manhood
A liar, his mouth
A night runner, his legs
And for a murderer, it is his heart

Why then not die to finish his grievances
Remove the eyes from the adulterer
Cut the hands of the thief
Chop off the spy's ears

A rapist cut off his manhood
And chop off the night runner's legs
As you seal the mouth of a liar
And remove the heart of the murderer

Tit for tat a fair game

US
In the beginning, 'twas respect
We gave her, with much love
With time, she gradually grew
In us, her fear was born
Larger and larger she became
As we slowly withdrew from her
She declared her wrath on us
Since then we recoil at her mention
She grows bigger and bigger
Like a ripe pumpkin ready to burst
So, is her aggressive power
Power is no more, as always we are fleeing
Slowly with time, resentment, hate is born
From our hearts as her face horrifies us
We ran away to take refuge
From the wrath that may befall us
Her smile, that of a cunning chameleon
But alas, those that eat with the devil
Can eat with her
Her shameless deeds and stubborn nature
Lead to this storm
A disaster, causing so much pain, harm
A crime called war on terror
How unlike humane human beings are
America that was, is not what it is

SOLDIER CRY

Every day, every night
I look up at the sky
And tell myself I will fly
I will stand up and fight
And this time I will be right
On my two feet I will stand tight

I look at the horizon
Stronger grows my vision
I will rise again to command
With all my might in my hand
I will strike again and again
To build a castle not in vain

Although now I growl like a hound
Although I am flat on the ground
My friends have ran away
My foes are feeling okay
I promise to have the last laugh
And make smooth what is rough
I will rise from down
When the night breaks and its dawn
I will stand on my two feet
And raise my sword above the heat
Like a man who had fallen
I shall not fall again to sell my peace
A soldier, I will soldier on

JERUSALEM

Humble city
Holy town
Why you now
Where man was meant

To stay in peace
In the alcoves of your shadow
Why seed of sorrows
Sowed by this terror
In your neutral sky
Where man was meant
To stay in peace
Under same sky
Blanket of same cloud
At no time is there
Silver lining that was meant to be
But fighting's, spilling blood
Why men die all times
Fighting for your recognition
Of religion based on useless, senseless
Claims of not reason
By Christians, Islam's and Jews
When all know, God, Allah and Yahweh are one

UNFAIR
Holding a gun and a shield, arrow and bullet
Readying to wipe out the innocent
And promote injustice

With my pen paper
To face the truth and right

This my weapon and shield
Will aid my fight against this

You fight with your hands
And I fight with my heart

You fight with a satanic mind
I fight with the will of God

I will write and will never tire of saying the truth
You will butcher and kill me and others
But truth kills
Kills the unjust
Even if am dead

THANK YOU

A gift from God given to me
Planning my life from birth to death
And I nothing to give in return
But to humble and respect you
Obedience to gain a handful more blessings

To see me excel in life
Encouragement and support
That made obstacles into strongholds
The security grant that I had from you
That makes me a winner not a loser

In sorrow you brought happiness
My failures you converted to victories
When I did wrong, you were ready to correct
And my achievements you always cheered
I curse the day that separates me from you

For all this, what shall I pay
How will I show my gratitude
Gold can't for what you sacrificed
Thank you, is what I can afford
And ask for God's blessings upon you
Thank you dad and mum

For Maurice and Lynnet Tabalia

LITTLE ROBIN HOOD

Young childish, just a baby
But an adventurer
Wearing black Indian moccasins
With a coat made from fur

With red folamy eyes
A small rifle on his shoulders
Walking towards the edge
Of a forest known for little terror

A hunter, with no shield
But a heart and a soul
That can hold both water and fire
From noon to moon, moon to noon

Rats scamper from him
And the small kids scatter
From this fiery flaming fiend
That kills with only a single look

BHAGDAD: CITY OF SINBAD

Oldest city
On us have pity
Sinbad and his sailor
Abunuwasi and tailors
Sultans and kings of Babylon
Their lives they carried on
For no invasions could conquer

The crowds cheered
While a few jeered
As we entered this town
Victory against their own

Bringing down the statue
Of the king with no virtue
And they clapped and tapped as it dropped

The big city, a city that is ruined
Everywhere terror reigned
We had celebrated victory
Too early judging from history
For victory ain't no victory till
The last enemy soldier , you kill
We had bragged, but to death field dragged

They kill us, for they are invisible
Suicidical and also inconvincible
The battleground is their home
This city, our tomb, and big dome
We lost this war
Because, it wasn't right, it was raw
For the time being, it is snipers and bombers.

THE FALL
We called him elephant
But out of his earshot
The unsung king, our school bully
A boy with astonishing strength and size
They say since birth
He'd never fallen down
So we moved by him
Not daring to cross his path

He was too stupid and foolish
But, we small men, geniuses
And teachers cowed by his strength
Applauding and acclaiming him

Amos Tabalia

He called the shots
And we small soldiers
Always at his hand
To execute his crazy and dangerous orders

Once I called him elephant
With his bare hands he smote me
And for ten days I cried blood
My left cheek still bares the evidence

Now he lies on the spring bed
A skeleton of his old self
The elephant is fallen
Mere bones, from a tiny virus

www.ingramcontent.com/pod-product-compliance
Lightning Source LLC
Chambersburg PA
CBHW030053170426
43197CB00010B/1501